Herald of Hope

The Chapel Car of Quinwood, West Virginia

Nancy Richmond

Copyright 2013
All Rights Reserved

Acknowledgments

First, I would like to thank Wilma Taylor, one of the authors of 'This Train is Bound for Glory' for her kind words and encouragement, for her information on the chapel car 'Herald of Hope' and especially for her willingness to share her photos with me.

Next, I would like to thank former Quinwood resident David Brown for finding and posting so many wonderful articles, pictures and books about the early days of Quinwood and the Herald of Hope on the internet, and for allowing me to use them.

Finally, I would like to offer my sincere appreciation to everyone who gave me permission to use their pictures of Quinwood, including but not limited to Bob Weaver, Sammy Jack Pomeroy, Martin Rudd, Pam Carroll Fitzwater, Troy Hunter, and Kimberly Adkins Spencer.

Also, although the copyright on many of the older photographs used in this book has run out and they have become public domain, and the identities of many of those people responsible for the pictures have been lost, I would like say thank you to all of the unnamed photographers who took so many wonderful pictures of the chapel cars and of Quinwood coal camp in its early years, which have allowed us to have a glimpse of those days from so long ago.

Dedication

*This book is dedicated with love to
my two favorite coal miners:*

Charles Richmond and Aldon George

Books by Nancy Richmond

William McClung- Appalachian Frontiersman

Grandfather Billie-A Greenbrier County Hero

Ghosts of Greenbrier County

Appalachian Folklore

Haunted Lewisburg

The Battle of Lewisburg

The History of an Appalachian Family

Contents

1. Quinwood Coal Camp   1

2. America's Chapel Cars   35

3. The Herald of Hope   65

4. Hope Comes to Quinwood   91

5. Legacy of Hope   111

Chapter One
Quinwood Coal Camp

Coal was first discovered in West Virginia in 1742. At that time the state was still a part of Virginia. Mining as a serious industry began in 1820, and by 1840 over three hundred thousand tons of coal were being mined in (West) Virginia every year.

Following the Civil War coal mining grew extensively. The demand for coal for homes, factories and especially for railroad steam engine trains was enormous. By the early 1900s, an average of one hundred and forty million tons of coal were being produced in West Virginia annually.

As the need for coal became more expedient, speculators sent mining engineers

Quinwood Coal Mines - 1920s

with the survey teams that mapped the area for the rail lines. These teams traveled further and further into the wild and mostly unsettled parts of the state, deep in the heart of the Appalachian Mountain range. In most cases, there were no established towns or even passable roads into the inhospitable territory.

The engineers, who hoped to locate large coal outcrops in Greenbrier County, were not disappointed. The positive reports that they submitted prompted the speculators to send their own prospect teams to investigate the territory. Each prospect team numbered twenty to thirty men, all mounted on horseback, with pack mules carrying supplies and equipment. The teams were composed mostly of laborers, men who used shovels and picks to clear work sites. Dynamite was used to remove stumps and large boulders from the area, and sometimes for the

Mining Light 'Lamp House' - Quinwood Mine

rudimentary mining that the teams would do. Everything the men needed they brought with them on their mules. Tents and cooking equipment, food, clothing and whatever else might be necessary during the weeks or even months that they were afield was carried in the canvas saddle packs.

Several mining engineers and at least one chemist, along with all their equipment, also accompanied each prospect team. The prospectors would dig test tunnels into the outcrops, with some tunnels running as much as fifty feet or more. It sometimes took months of prospecting before a suitable location for advanced mining would be found.

When the rich Sewell coal seam was discovered along at the head waters of Meadow Creek in the northwest mountains of Greenbrier County, little of the area had ever been explored.

Main Street in Quinwood

The territory was virtually a wilderness. Only a few logging endeavors and a handful of hardy mountain men had ever journeyed into that part of the county.

The elevation of the land under which the Sewell seam was buried was nearly three thousand feet, making it one of the highest spots in the state, and most of the acreage was located on a western facing slope, which meant that it regularly received large amounts of snowfall when northwestern winds carried moisture from the great lakes up the mountains.

Snow drifts of over three feet were not uncommon, and the other harsh features of the terrain had kept the area virtually uninhabited until the beginning of the 1900s.

The few mountain folk who did manage to eek out a living by farming or logging in the hostile and unforgiving region along Meadow

Building the Quinwood Bank

Creek dubbed the territory 'little Alaska' because of the relentless blizzards and heavy snows that sometimes lay on the ground from late October until early May.

The Gauley Mountain Company owned the rights to the Sewell coal seam on Meadow Creek. When large coal reserves were found in 1918, they leased the land to six mine operators.

A few years earlier brothers John and Tom Raine, the founders of Rainelle, had built a twenty mile section of railway that ran from the main lines of the C&O Railroad up to the turnpike that lay at the bottom of Big Sewell mountain. There they constructed a large band mill which eventually became the Meadow River Lumber Company, the largest mill of its kind in the world.

Their railroad continued on for several miles north to the Meadow River in order to

Quinwood Store - 1920s

carry timber from the mountains to the mill. The six new mines would be responsible for building their own railway branch up the creek and connecting it to the mine tipples so that the coal could be loaded and shipped down to the C&O railroad for disbursement to buyers.

Quinn Morton and W.S. Wood had acquired one of the leases to the Sewell coal seam which was located five miles beyond the end of the railroad, and in 1919 they started a mine under the name of the Imperial Smokeless Coal Company.

A crew was organized to build a railroad branch into the area, and the new section of track was called the Greenbrier and Eastern Railroad. The rail line was completed in 1920. Before that time all lumber and supplies for the new coal camp had to be hauled over the Big Mountain road from Rupert, WV.

Early Days of Quinwood

Quinn and Wood set up a portable saw mill at the foot of the mountain to make boards to construct housing for the miners, and began hauling supplies up an old county road to the site of their newly established mining camp, which they named Quinwood.

Even before any of the houses for the hundreds of miners that would be needed to work for the company were built, enterprising men began traveling up the rough paths made by the railroad crews into Quinwood.

The first resident of the coal camp was George Washington George, who built a small lean-to on the edge of the lease property. He was quickly hired and put to work clearing out brush from the site of the proposed mine road. Another young man found a wooden piano box at the train depot in Rainelle and begged the work train to haul it up the mountain so that he

Quinwood Steam Train

could live in it until the coal camp houses were built. By 1920 the town was filling up, and the first general store (owned by Erskine Nutter), and the Quinwood Post Office began operations.

With six new mines being opened in the area, the lease owners knew that they would need a bank to make payrolls and finance their enterprises. John Wade Bell and W.S. Wood hired John Nuttall, a young man who had been a surveyor, a mine inspector and a Circuit Clerk, to manage the Bank of Quinwood.

The bank was originally located in a small shack and Nuttall was its sole employee. Whenever Nuttall could not work, the entire bank was closed until such time as he could return. However, the enterprise thrived and during its second year of business moved into a steel and concrete building that was located along the narrow unpaved county road. The

First Quinwood Resident GW George & Family

multi-storied 'skyscraper' also housed several other businesses, including a barber shop and the office of Doctor J. G. Leech, the town's first physician.

More and more shops soon appeared along the county road, which became the main street of the coal camp. Main Street eventually housed several hotels, restaurants and grocery stores.

A small train depot was constructed beside the railroad tracks, which were located at the eastern end of the camp. Almost everything that came into the town was brought in on the train. Near the depot, Ratha Trout opened a livery and blacksmith shop, needed by many residents of the town who continued to own horses well into the middle of the century.

The camp continued to expand and eventually Quinwood encompassed an area

Charlie Smith at the Quinwood Train Depot

of just over one square mile. The little town was completely encircled by the wilderness for miles in every direction.

Dozens of coal camp houses, small structures that had only a few rooms, quickly appeared on the sides of the mountain near the coal mine. Still, the builders could not keep up with the housing needs of the large number of men who were migrating to the new camp, and numerous tents could be seen along the perimeters of the rapidly growing town.

Several large boarding houses were hastily constructed along the county road, where single men could rent a sleeping space. They immediately filled up with workers who were hoping to find employment in the mines.

Because there was no transportation for the miners up to the site of the mining operation, the camp houses were all built as close to the

Quinwood Commercial District

work site as possible, so the men could reach the 'entry' easily. The mine entrance was a 'drift mouth' type, which meant that a hole was dug into the side of the mountain where the coal seam lay. As the coal was mined, the hole descended further and further under the ground.

The coal seam was usually five or six feet in height, and was dug out twelve to fourteen feet in width. Wooden posts were used to shore up the roof of the mine, and mine rails ran into the mine along one side of the coal. A cutting machine drove into the 'face' or front of the coal seam, where miners harvested the coal and loaded it into cars which ran outside and dumped their loads.

By 1920 most larger mines, like the one at Quinwood, used cutting machines powered by electricity, which was produced by a steam powered generator at the mine site. The job

Completed Quinwood Bank (Left)

was a dirty and dangerous one, and only paid around forty three cents a day. Boys as young as twelve years old were often hired to do menial jobs in the mine.

As was usual in the coal camps of the 1900s, the mining company owned almost everything. All of the housing was the property of the company and could only be rented by men who worked at the mines.

If a man lost his job due to poor performance or illness, or even because of an injury he received at work, he was forced to move out of the company house so that a new miner could take his place. The men received their meager wages in the form of script, which was a type of money printed or minted by the individual mine operators.

The largest store in every mining camp was the 'Company Store' which was owned and

Blacksmith Ratha Trout (left) and Family

operated by the mining company. Workers could shop at the company store on credit, and their rent and any bill they owed to the store was held out of their earnings before they received it, so that by the time pay day arrived, most of the men already owed all their wages back to the company, keeping them forever in debt.

The men who moved to Quinwood in order to work in the mines were a rugged and independent group. Many were either the children of immigrants or were immigrants themselves. Most were of Scotts-Irish or Italian descent. Often the Italian families changed their names when coming to the United States, because they were afraid of being discriminated against by Americans.

In the first years after the town was founded, most of the miners were single men with no families. They lived either in the local

Mountainside Homes in Quinwood

boarding facilities or with one of the few families who were renting company houses.

Several saloons and bordellos sprang up in the rough mining camp, giving the local miners, loggers and railroad men a place to spend time and relax during the few hours that they were not working or sleeping. Almost every one of the men in the camp carried a gun, despite the severe gun laws which had been enacted in the state because of the large number of murders that took place in the more remote areas of West Virginia.

Quinwood banker John Nuttall often repeated a conversation that he had held with Fayette County Deputy Sheriff Elias Hatfield (son of Anderson 'Devil Anse' Hatfield of the Hatfield/McCoy feud.) Nuttall said *"Elias preached to all of us to carry no gun unless it be a .38, saying "If you hit a man in a vital place*

Housing for Miners

with anything of a lesser caliber than a .38 that man will have several seconds of life left in him to give him time to kill you before he drops, but a .38 will knock him out at once, therefore if you do not have a .38 you had best not start any shooting."

Nuttall's opinion of most mining camp murders was that " *It was seldom that a man murdered anybody unless the victim was a buddy or a close friend. Two good friends would drink enough whisky to lose their reason, one would accuse the other of cheating in a card game or of stealing a girl or a bank lamp, to start a fight that would end in the death of one of them.*"

Like many other coal camps in the area, Quinwood soon acquired the reputation of being an uncivilized and dangerous place in which to live, especially for women and children.

Quinwood Mine Supervisor's House

In less than three years nearly four hundred men were employed by the Imperial Smokeless Coal Company. As more family housing became available, miners sent for their wives and children to join them. When the first baby was born in the coal camp, his proud parents named him Quinwood Farren.

The harsh and rugged territory of western Greenbrier County was a barrier to the formation of a church in the isolated coal camp, and no pastor could be found that was willing to begin a permanent congregation there. Any time that a marriage, baptism or funeral was held, it was necessary to have a preacher from another town make the arduous journey through the mountainous terrain to Quinwood.

Although the community was in dire need of a church, it would not be until the spring of 1922 that their prayers would be answered.

County Road Through Quinwood

It was in that year that Quinwood would become home to one of a handful of specially made missionary railroad car churches that traveled the country bringing religion to people who lived in isolated and inaccessible areas. They were known as America's Chapel Cars.

Episcopalian 'Northern Michigan' Chapel Car

Chapter Two
America's Chapel Cars

With the coming of the Industrial Revolution and the growth of the railroads throughout America, Christian religions saw an opportunity to expand their ministries to the people of the nation who lived in rural and formerly unreachable areas.

The Baptist, Episcopal and Catholic denominations all built specially fitted railroad cars called chapel cars to provide religious services and to help establish new churches wherever they were needed. The chapel cars also held revivals and gave encouragement in towns where churches had already been built but were not growing.

From the 1890s until the end of the 1930s, there were over a dozen chapel cars that

Baptist Chapel Car 'Good Will'

toured the country, spreading the gospel to those who lived near the railroad tracks. The chapel cars took the place of the earlier circuit preachers who once traveled the country on horseback, holding church services in the backwoods areas of America.

On record there were seven American Baptist Publication Society cars: Evangel, Emmanuel, Glad Tidings, Good Will, Messenger of Peace, Herald of Hope and Grace. There were three Catholic Extension Society cars: St. Anthony, St. Peter, and St. Paul. There were also three Episcopal cars: The Cathedral Car of North Dakota, Chapel Car 1 of Upper Michigan and Chapel Car 2 of Upper Michigan, making a total of thirteen missionary chapel cars.

All of the cars were designed to provide both a section for holding religious services and a ten by sixteen foot living quarters for the

Baptist Chapel Car 'Messenger of Peace'

missionary family. Although the interior design of the chapel cars varied, each was equipped with an alter, pews and stained glass windows. The chapel cars were not owned by the railroad companies, instead they were each privately funded by members of their respective religions.

The Baptist Chapel Cars: The American Baptist Publication Society had several wealthy pastors, including Boston Smith, Charles Colby and Colgate Hoyt. These three men donated the funds to build the first Baptist chapel car, the Evangel.

Colgate Hoyt also organized other businessmen into what was called the 'Baptist Chapel Car Syndicate'. A group of well known businessmen belonged to the syndicate, which was headed by John D. Rockefeller.

All seven of the Baptist chapel cars were manufactured by the Barney & Smith Company,

Catholic Chapel Car 'St. Anthony'

and were constructed during the time period from 1891 through 1913. Inventor Thomas A. Edison was very interested in the program, and donated one of his newly invented gramophones for each of the Baptist cars.

'Evangel' was dedicated by the church on May 23, 1891 at the Cincinnati Grand Central Depot. The chapel car's first journey took it to St. Paul, Minnesota, where church members donated an organ for the car. It traveled on to Montana and then to Oregon, spreading the gospel among the small towns and villages that lay along path of the railroad.

In 1892 Evangel served in Minnesota and Wisconsin, and in 1894 was sent to the southern part of the country. From 1901 until 1924, the mission car was called to serve throughout the western states of Oklahoma, Texas, Kansas, Colorado and Nebraska.

Baptist Chapel Car 'Glad Tidings'

Eventually, the aging car was retired to Rawlins, Wyoming, where it was incorporated into the design of a local Baptist church.

'Emmanuel', the second Baptist chapel car, was built during the financial panic of 1893. For this reason many of the items that went into the making of the car were donated by various corporations.

Emmanuel was a much larger car that Evangel had been, and was almost seventy feet in length. It was dedicated in Denver Colorado on May 24, 1893.

Rev. Wheeler and his wife were the first missionaries to serve on Emmanuel. The train that was bringing the chapel car home in 1895 was involved in a wreck, and Rev.Wheeler was killed. As a memorial, a special stained glass window was created and mounted in the living quarters of the car.

Episcopalian Chapel Car 'North Dakota'

Emmanuel was sent to minister to the towns in the western and northwestern states until 1938. After sitting unused on a railroad spur in South Fork, Colorado for several years, it was donated to a Baptist camp at Swan Lake, South Dakota. Eventually the chapel car was used as a storage bin for an engineering company, until it was bought by a carpenter from the Prairie Village Park, who fully restored it. Emmanuel is now on the National Register of Historic Places.

The chapel car 'Glad Tidings' was dedicated in Saratoga, New York, on May 25, 1894. Reverend Rust and his young bride were the first missionaries appointed to it. They remained with Glad Tidings long enough for two of their five children to be born in the car.

Glad Tidings traveled on the Chicago, Burlington and Quincy Railroad to several

Baptist Chapel Car 'Emmanuel'

destinations in the Midwestern states. In 1905, it was sent to Colorado, Arizona and Wyoming. During World War I, the car was forced to set on the sidelines in Douglas, Wyoming for the duration of the conflict, and served there.

In 1920 Glad Tidings was reassigned to Arizona. In 1926 the train made its final stop in Flagstaff, where the wheels were removed and it was placed on a foundation and became the Glad Tidings Baptist Church. It was eventually dismantled in 1930.

'Goodwill' was dedicated in Saratoga Springs, New York on June 1, 1895. It was sent to Texas and worked in conjunction with the Texas Baptist Convention. The chapel car was in Galveston during the 1900 hurricane. It was damaged and required special donations from Texas Baptist congregations in order to be repaired before continuing its mission.

Interior of Baptist Chapel Car 'Emmanuel'

In 1905, the car was sent to Missouri and Colorado, and was then transferred to the western states, where it traveled the rails for twenty years in the service of the church. In 1938 the car was retired and parked behind a hotel in Boyes Hot Springs, California, where it sat until 1998. It was then purchased by a local businessman who had it restored.

'Messenger of Peace' was often referred to as the 'ladies car' because it was built with donations from seventy five Baptist women. The manufacturer of the car, Barney & Smith, agreed to build the car at cost if the women could raise the funds. Messenger of Peace was dedicated on May 21, 1898 in Rochester, New York. It traveled through the Midwestern states until 1910, then it was commissioned for use by the Young Mens Christian Association for one year. In 1913, the car was sent out to the Pacific

Catholic Chapel Car 'St. Peter'

Northwest, where it worked in the state of Washington during World War One. The car was retired and turned into a diner after being sold to a local business.

Later it was sold to a private owner who used it for storage. In 1997 the old chapel car was donated to the Northwest Railway Museum, where it was restored to its original condition.

'Herald of Hope' was the final Baptist chapel car to be constructed of wood. It was called 'The Young Men's Car' because the men of the Woodward Baptist Church in Detroit donated one thousand dollars towards its building fund. Herald of Hope was dedicated in Detroit on May 27, 1900. It originally served in the Midwestern states. In 1911, the car was reconditioned at the Barney & Smith factory in Dayton, Ohio, and in 1915 the Herald of Hope was transported to West Virginia to serve in the

Interior of Catholic Chapel Car 'St. Paul'

states' lumber and coal camps. Rev. William Newton and his wife were the missionaries during that time. They stayed with the car until Rev. Newton's death in 1931. His wife Fanny considered the car her home, and lived in it until 1935. The church lost touch with the car until 1947, until it was learned that it had been retired and used as a mine office in Quinwood, WV.

'Grace' was the last of the Baptist chapel cars that was built. It was the only car of its type to be constructed of steel. The funds to build the car were donated by the Conaway family in memory of their daughter Grace.

Grace was built in 1915 and cost five times as much to manufacture as the first of the Baptist chapel cars. It was much larger and had better living quarters for the missionaries. The car was dedicated in Los Angles in 1915 and served in California, then continued on to

Baptist Chapel Car 'Glad Tidings'

Nevada, Utah, Wyoming and Colorado. Eventually, Grace was placed on permanent display at the American Baptist Assembly, which is located at Green Lake, Wisconsin.

The Roman Catholic Chapel Cars:

Father Francis Kelley became the president of the Catholic Church Extension in 1905. He had taken a tour of the Baptist chapel car Messenger of Peace, and was impressed with what the car had been able to do for the Baptist faith. Because the mission of the Catholic Church Extension was to bring the Catholic religion to those in remote areas, he felt that chapel cars would be able to offer services like those of the Baptists to people of his own denomination.

Father Kelley appealed to members of his church, saying "If the Baptists can do it, why not the Catholics?" The funds for three chapel cars were subsequently donated for the endeavor.

Interior of the Baptist Chapel Car 'Grace'

The first was built by Barney & Smith, but the two following cars were manufactured by the Pullman Company.

'St. Anthony' was the first Catholic chapel car. It was larger than the Baptist cars, measuring over seventy two feet in length. It was dedicated and blessed by the church in 1907, and served in Kansas, Louisiana, Mississippi, and in the West and Pacific Northwest. In 1909 it was sent to Oregon, where it helped to create more than eighty Catholic parishes. It was eventually retired when the railroads would no longer transport wooden passenger cars.

The Catholic chapel car 'St. Peter' was made of steel and at the time was the longest railroad car in the world. It was in service from 1912 until 1930, and traveled throughout the Midwest, establishing many new churches.

Baptist Chapel Car 'Glad Tidings'

It was placed in storage in 1936.

'St. Paul' was the last and largest of the Catholic chapel cars. It measured an astounding eighty six feet in length, and was made of steel. It was manufactured at the Pullman Company. St. Paul served in Louisiana, Texas, North Carolina and Oklahoma.

The chapel car was placed in storage with the St. Peter in 1936, before being sold to Charles Bovey, a Montana Senator, for his railroad museum. Later it was traded to the Escanaba-Lake Superior Railroad.

The Episcopal Chapel Cars: William Walker was appointed the Episcopal Bishop of North Dakota in 1883, making him the overseer of an enormous territory that had only a few isolated towns and villages.

After taking a tour of a European chapel car, Bishop Walker became convinced that

Chapel Car 'St. Peter' In Winter

they would be the most efficient way for him to reach the people in his diocese, and he began asking for donations from his flock in order to have a chapel car built. The car was called the Church of the Advent-The Cathedral Car of North Dakota.

'Church of the Advent' measured sixty feet in length and had two sections, one for worship and one for living quarters for the missionary. It began its service in North Dakota on November 13, 1890.

The car was able to travel the rails without cost because the local railroad companies agreed to pull it from place to place at no charge to the church. Walker himself was the first missionary to serve on the chapel car. It was retired in 1899 at Carrington, North Dakota. It had traveled over seventy thousand miles doing mission work in the state.

Catholic Chapel Car 'St. Paul'

'The Chapel Cars of Northern Michigan' were commissioned by Bishop Mott Williams, head of the diocese of Northern Michigan. He was faced with problems similar to those of Bishop Walker when trying to serve the people of his diocese.

Although Willams could not raise the funds to have new chapel cars built, he managed to purchase two passenger railroad cars that had been retired. He had these converted into chapel cars, which he used in service of his territory from 1891 to 1898.

Not only did the two chapel cars travel throughout Michigan during that time period, one was used as a temporary church for three years when a fire destroyed most of the town of Ontonagon, Michigan in 1898. At length, both of the Chapel Cars of Northern Michigan were retired and later sold by the church.

Sunday Morning Services

Chapter Three
The Herald of Hope

The sixth Baptist chapel car, Herald of Hope, was dedicated in Detroit, Michigan on May 27, 1900. Something occurred during the ceremony that was unique to all the chapel cars. While Dr. Wayland Hoyt was offering up a prayer, a beautiful white dove was seen flying above the car. Just as it reached the point directly above the Dr. Hoyt, it slowed and circled the area several times. All those who saw it thought that it was a miraculous sight.

The Herald of Hope began its service in Michigan. It was assigned a three part mission to accomplish for the church. The first was to bring the Baptist religion to places that had no church and help establish one, the second was to provide support and religious services to the

Miners Meeting on 'Herald of Hope'

railroad workers on the trains that transported the chapel car, and the third was to aid Baptist churches that were struggling to stay afloat.

Charles Rosecrans and his wife were the first missionaries to serve on the Herald of Hope. In the summer of 1900 the young couple made a stop in Grindstone City in Michigan. There they helped organize a Baptist church, the first in the town. The chapel car moved on to Melvin, but the young pastor became ill and had to be replaced by Reverend E. S. Wilson, who traveled with the Herald of Hope to Brown City in November of 1901.

Unfortunately, Wilson also became sick and had to leave the Herald of Hope. A much older missionary couple, the Reverend W. W. Dewey and his wife, were appointed to continue on with the chapel car.

Their first trip took the missionaries to

After Services on 'Herald of Hope'

Cement City, Michigan, where they helped to bolster a floundering church. Under their guidance, several new churches were organized in Michigan towns along the railroads, and numerous revivals were held in others.

Eventually Rev. Dewey was given his own church to pastor in Detroit, and in 1902 Reverend A. P. McDonald became the fourth missionary for the Herald of Hope. He served throughout Michigan until 1907.

The next pastoral couple appointed to the car was Rev. Walter Sparks and his wife Katherine. Together they traveled on the Herald of Hope through the states of Illinois and Iowa from 1908 until 1911. At that time, the chapel car was over ten years old and in need of several repairs, so it was recalled to the Barney & Smith factory to be overhauled, refitted and repainted before continuing its mission.

Interior of 'Herald of Hope'

The Herald of Hope was rededicated to its work in a ceremony at Dayton, Ohio on November 28, 1911. Rev. Sparks and his wife then continued with the car into the state of Ohio, holding services in Brewster, New Boston, Columbus and Portsmith, before being sent across the Mississippi River into Iowa.

In 1915 the chapel car, now fifteen years old, was dispatched once more to Dayton, Ohio to be refitted. When it was again ready to take to the rails, the Herald of Hope was assigned to serve in West Virginia.

Reverend Sparks and his wife were given a six months hiatus from the mission field, and Rev. William F. Newton and his wife Fanny were assigned as temporary missionaries on the chapel car during their absence.

Newton was a native of Rhode Island and had been a missionary in Connecticut and

Chapel Car Bible Stand

out west on several Indian reservations.

West Virginia at that time was in dire need of assistance. Roscoe Keeney, a Baptist historian, wrote that the Herald of Hope was the answer to a prayer for the people of the state. *"Isolated from one another by mountains, winter snows and heavy rains, West Virginians wanted help.....The chapel car, which came a few years later, was a perfect response."*

The Herald of Hope began its voyage into West Virginia in Point Pleasant, then traveled on to Henderson and Wheeling. Reverend Newton proved to be an unorthodox but effective preacher. He regularly went into the pool halls in the towns where they were stationed and preached to the local men.

Reverend Newton often spoke of how the men would stop their games, politely lay down their pool cues and listen attentively as

'Herald of Hope' at Wallace, WV

talked, and would invite him to return and speak to them again.

The Herald of Hope spent the summer of 1915 traveling on the railroad tracks of West Virginia, stopping in Wallace, Lumberport, Industrial, Haywood and Burnsville. Whenever the weather was too hot for the congregation to be comfortable inside, Reverend Newton would give his sermon from the rear vestibule of the Herald of Hope, while his listeners either stood or sat nearby.

The Newtons left the chapel car for a short vacation and did not expect to return to it, but when Reverend Sparks was assigned to a different area, William and Fanny agreed to take his place, and the Herald of Hope became their home for the next seventeen years.

The Herald of Hope, as were the five Baptist chapel cars before it, was constructed of

Chapel Car Vestibule

wood, and had an open vestibule at both ends. The interior was divided into two parts, a living area for the missionaries and the chapel.

The living quarters consisted of a small room located at one end of the car. It contained a bed and chest of drawers on one side and a stove, china cabinet, table, chairs, sideboard and a sink that was connected to an overhead water tank on the other side.

The chapel section of the car was much larger. There were pews on each side of a narrow aisle, large enough to seat three people on one side and two on the other, which provided seating for around seventy five people. Next to the boarding door there was a small closet and a Deacon's bench. The car had a beautiful Estey pump organ in the front section. The domed ceiling was fitted with large brass chandeliers. Above the regulation railroad car

Chapel Car Living Quarters

windows were panes of stained glass that gave the car the illusion of being a regular church. Although the accommodations seem cramped by today's standards, most of the missionaries who lived in a chapel car stated that it quickly became their home.

From 1915 to 1918 the Newtons traveled through West Virginia. The car stopped at Gassaway, Clay, Hurricane, Smithers, Gauley Bridge, Boomer, Cedar Grove, Belle and Cabin Creek. In each of these towns the Newtons gave aid to Baptist churches that were struggling to become more productive and gain members, which was one of the missions assigned to the car.

The Newtons also fulfilled another of the missions of the Herald of Hope, which was to minister to the numerous railroad workers that transported the Baptist chapel car from one

West Virginia Railroad Workers

destination to another. From the conception of the chapel car system, most railroad companies had instructed their engineers to convey the cars to various locations at no cost to the church organizations that owned them.

In return, the missionaries held services for the railway workers whenever they were side-tracked. Each day at noon and again at midnight (for the men working the late shift) the pastor would hold a short service that most of the workers attended during their dinner break, listening to the sermon while they ate. The missionary leader often played music on the car's gramophone or sang a solo before delivering his message.

Many of the railroad men dedicated their lives to Christ and then joined the Chapel Car Railroad Temperance Society, which was begun when the first chapel cars were built.

Elk and Little Kanawha Railroad

In the spring of 1917, the Herald of Hope stopped in Frametown, WV. Bob Weaver recounts the visit on his internet website at hurherald.com. He says " Annie Harvey Dulaney wrote in the December 1976 edition of the Braxton County Historical County Journal that " *It was sometime in 1912, exact date unknown, that train service was begun on the Elk and Little Kanawha (railway). So, the train service came, changing our lives in many ways. In order to get a right of way, it had to be made a public carrier, taking on both passengers and freight, thus we had transportation to and from Frametown, Gasaway and Rosedale. Then, too, the camps showed a life that we had not known before.*

The railway, along with the timbering and millwork, provided good wages for several men during its stay. It brought peddlers,

Hauling Supplies for the Railroad

hoboes, and drummers, all following the camps.

The days of the Elk and Little Kanawha narrow gauge slipped by. In our own environment and in the outside world things were happening. Better roads in, some places were being built, conveniences such as telephones, and washing machines were in use.

The chapel car, Herald of Hope, brought by Rev. And Mrs. Newton, stopped on a railroad siding at Frametown. A revival was held, and the Baptist Church there was reorganized and named Hope Baptist Church.

All charter members of that new organization are now deceased. The last two survivors were Mrs. Maggie Wood and my mother Georgia Harvey."

The Newtons left Frametown and the Herald of Hope continued its long journey

Railroad Workers Service on 'Herald of Hope'

through the more isolated areas of West Virginia, stopping in Dunbar, Malden and Dana, then on to Quincy, Boomer and Clay, which were all coal mining camps.

At the beginning of World War One, the Herald of Hope and all of the chapel cars were moved onto side rails where they spent the duration of the conflict. The Newtons found themselves stranded in the Dunbar/Nitro area, but it proved to be a blessing in disguise, for the large munitions plants in the area employed thousands of people who came to the services on the little chapel car, seeking hope and encouragement during the war torn years.

Several times during that period, Rev. Newton managed to persuade the local rail companies to move the Herald of Hope into the Cabin Creek area, where he spent a few days each time preaching to the local miners. The

Estey Pump Organ from 'Herald of Hope'

coal camps were suffering terribly from both the mining strikes and the floods which had been happening all along the railroads. On one such trip, angry miners tried to dynamite the chapel car. On another, according to Rev. Newman, *"The devil put up a great howl. Men stood in their store doors with clenched fists, telling us to go right on through. I went from store to store, bought a little here and there and invited my knockers to come to the meeting that night. Some came; others followed."*

Eventually, the war ended, and the government once again opened the railroads for public use. The Herald of Hope was given a new assignment and the chapel car returned to the railways and began its journey though some of the most wild and unexplored areas of the Appalachian mountain region, into the newly formed coal camp of Quinwood.

Winter Service on 'Herald of Hope'

Chapter Four
Hope Comes To Quinwood

The Herald of Hope chapel car with the missionary couple of Rev. William Newton and his wife Fanny arrived in Quinwood coal camp just before dawn on the morning of September 15, 1922. The aging car was placed on a sideline near the Quinwood train depot at the bottom of the camp's main street.

Quinwood at that time was a bustling little self contained village of some three or four hundred people, mostly miners who worked for the Quinwood Imperial Smokeless Coal Company, or for one of the businesses that supported it.

Most of the housing for miners had been built on the hillsides adjacent to the mines, and the numerous dirt roads running between the

Winter in Quinwood - 1920s

buildings gave the landscape an odd, jumbled look. The houses were small, and used oil lamps for lighting. The miners invariably had coal stoves in their homes for both heating and cooking. If they were lucky, they had screen wire to cover the windows during the summer so that they could be left open for ventilation. There was no indoor plumbing, so for each house that was constructed, a small outhouse was built in the back yard for that family's use. There were community water pumps from which to draw water, set at a distance of about forty feet apart, so that each pump served the four or five houses closest to it.

Prohibition laws had been in force for several years by the time the Newton's came to minister to the coal camp, but home made moon shine was much in evidence, and there were several saloons in town that still openly sold

Reverend William Newton

it to their customers. So while some people welcomed the chapel car, others saw it as an invasion of their way of life.

The missionaries were seen as outsiders for some time, and since there were no churches in the town, they had to begin to build their congregation from the bottom up. Reverend Newton soon became known as 'the chapel car man' in the area, and it was not long before the people in the coal camp came to admire him for his simple and honest ways.

In one of his early sermons, the pastor told how his father had joined the Union army during the Civil War and had never come home. His mother had remarried and his step father drove him away from his family when he was only twelve years old. His heartbroken mother had called after him as he left *"Willie, be a good boy. Keep good company, and it will all come*

The Quinwood Hotel

out all right in the end." Rev. Newton concluded his sermon by saying "*My mother's prayers have followed me the whole world through.*" The fact that Newton too had lived a hard life went a long way in endearing him to the miners of Quinwood

The pastor and his wife Fanny were well liked by the local children. The missionaries welcomed them to the Herald of Hope whenever they came by, whether it was time for church services or not. One of Fanny Newton's favorite visitors was little Lucille Pomeroy (Fox), who began coming to the chapel car with her father and older sister when she was only a year old. She never forgot being carried to the car by her father. Lucille often talked of what a good influence Mrs. Newton was in their lives, and how she showed the girls how to dress and act like ladies. Mrs. Newton later taught Lucille's

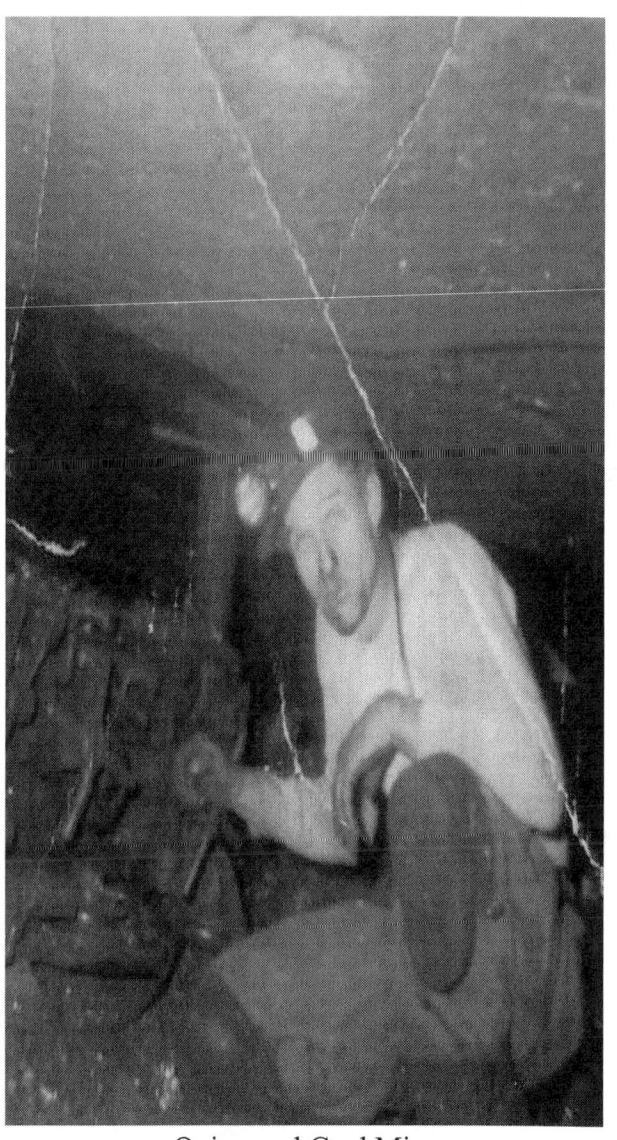

Quinwood Coal Miner

sister how to play the chapel car organ, and helped to buy a Baldwin piano for them.

The townspeople came to like and respect the Newtons, and accepted them as valued members of the community. Soon the weekly services at the Herald of Hope were full to overflowing.

Life was harsh and unforgiving in the coal camp, but the Newtons brought hope in the form of their sermons and in their actions, which created a social awareness and community spirit in the residents of Quinwood that is still in evidence to this day.

The outpouring of kindness and generosity from the congregation encouraged the Newtons to the degree that they felt the time had come to construct a permanent church for the chapel car members. It would be the first church in the town, so it decided that it would

Virgie and Walter George with Aldon and Olive

be christened the First Baptist Church of Quinwood.

By January of 1924 the dedicated congregation the Herald of Hope chapel car had raised eight thousand dollars. Construction of the church began on a large lot at the top of the hill on the main street of Quinwood. The building was completed in 1925, and its members adopted a charter for the newly established Baptist organization.

One of the first people to sign the charter was Virgie (Cales) George. Virgie was the wife of Walter George, the oldest son of the town's first resident, George Washington George. Virgie and her children, Aldon and Olive, had regularly attended services in the chapel car, and now did the same at the new church.

Many others followed suit, including

Quinwood Movie Theater

the rough and hardened men who worked in the depths of the coal mines. The little country church formed a bond between the townspeople which has never been broken. It became a meeting place for the inhabitants of the coal camp, and many good deeds were done by its members over the years.

Reverend Newton and his wife Fanny continued to make the chapel car their home until 1931. At that time the pastor died while undergoing emergency surgery in Baltimore, Maryland, where he and his wife had been vacationing.

Reverend Newton was buried in Orange, Massachusetts, which was his wife's home town. Stricken by his loss, every business in Quinwood closed down operations on the day of his burial.

Fanny Newton returned to the Herald of Hope after her husband's funeral, and to the

First Baptist Church of Quinwood - 1920s

coal camp that she now considered her home.

In 1932 the owners of the chapel car, the American Baptist Publication Society, wanted to send the Herald of Hope to the nearby coal camp of Marfrance, where it would be placed on a stone foundation and used as a church for the community. Mrs. Newton refused to leave her home, and she was allowed to live in the car until 1935, when she finally moved to back to Massachusetts.

The Herald of Hope was sold for one dollar to the West Virginia Baptist Convention. It was moved to Marfrance as planned, where it stayed until after 1939, when a new church was built there. Eventually the chapel car was retired from service, and was bought by the Imperial Smokeless Coal Company. The car was moved back to Quinwood, where it was used as a mine office until the company closed. It was then side

Marfrance Coal Camp Church

railed on the tracks near the Quinwood train depot and stood empty for several years.

Retired Pastor David Brown, who grew up in Quinwood, remembers: *"The chapel car 'Herald of Hope' had been moved to a side track beyond the tipple at Quinwood when I used to visit it in the 1950s. It was about one half to three quarters of a mile beyond Red Parr's place at the bottom of the hill where Quinwood's business district was located. I remember going with the Quinwood Bible School each year to the site where the chapel car spent its last days. We would walk down the aisle of the chapel car and then have a picnic lunch beside it."*

Several years later, the land where the coal company once stood was reclaimed. The Herald of Hope was scrapped; and thus the chapel car passed into history.

Final Days of the 'Herald of Hope' Chapel Car

In 1995 Lucille Pomeroy Fox talked with Wilma and Norman Taylor, authors of "This Train is Bound For Glory - The Story of America's Chapel Cars" when they visited Quinwood in search of the chapel car. *Lucille reminisced , "When Mrs. Newton moved back to her home east, Mr. Bells had the car moved to the coal company and used it as an office. I'm sure they tried to keep an eye on it, because Mr. Bell thought a lot of that car. One time someone got in and set fire to it. Then I think they used it for storage or something. I will never forget that car. You know I spent most of my early years there. Mrs. Newton taught me how to act and dress. Almost everything I learned about my faith, I learned there...I can remember all the books, and the lights from all the lamps...and the music...and Mr. and Mrs. Newton."*

The First Baptist Church of Quinwood

Chapter Five
Legacy of Hope

The beacon of hope that was lit when the missionary chapel car first arrived in Quinwood in 1922 has continued to burn brightly through the years. In 1947, at a time when other small coal camps were dying off and becoming ghost towns, Quinwood applied for legal status and became an incorporated town in the state of West Virginia.

The Herald of Hope's legacy to the people of Quinwood is a commitment to community service that was instilled in the mountain people by Rev. Newton and his wife Fanny.

Through the years the residents of the town have been among the first in the area to respond to any type of emergency, whether it

Quinwood Volunteer Fire Department - 1950s

was due to floods, fires or mining disasters.

The Quinwood Volunteer Fire Department has served the town for over fifty years, depending entirely on the dedicated men and women who give freely of their time and risk their lives with no thought of reward other than to insure the safety of those in their charge.

The fire department also carries on a unique local tradition that was started many years ago to help the area's needy children. During the mid 1900s many of the families of miners could not afford to have Christmas, so the members of the Quinwood Volunteer Fire Department took up donations and bought a variety of apples, oranges, nuts and candy. The treats were placed in brown paper bags and were delivered to the house of every boy and girl in Quinwood and the surrounding towns by the fire department, accompanied by Santa Claus

Quinwood Emergency Ambulance Service

himself, riding atop the Quinwood fire truck. Santa still delivers his brown paper bags filled with treats every year in Quinwood, and 'Santa on the fire truck' is a treasured memory for every child who grew up there.

The Quinwood Emergency Ambulance Service is another business which serves the local population, providing help in almost any emergency. The experienced employees are never too busy to stop and volunteer aid or advice, or check the temperature or blood pressure of locals whenever they are needed.

Many of the citizens of Quinwood today are descendants of the original settlers. The Hilltop Restaurant, famous for its West Virginia style hots dogs topped with chili and slaw, has been owned and operated by the McClung family for three generations. Terry Beavers, owner of the town's newly opened Appalachian General

'Fire Truck Santa' Giving Christmas Treats

Store, is the daughter and granddaughter of Quinwood grocery store owners.

The saloons and pool halls that once lined the streets of the coal camp have long since been replaced with organizations like the Quinwood Community Food Pantry, which supplies food for needy families, and Hope Haven, a men's homeless shelter. In almost every aspect of the lives of the community's residents, helping someone less fortunate than themselves plays a factor.

The First Baptist Church of Quinwood, the offspring of the Herald of Hope chapel car, continues to care for its members and for the town. Two grandsons of George Washington George, first resident of the coal camp, have served at the church. Ronald George was the custodian of the sanctuary and eventually was licensed by the church as a minister. Another

First Baptist Church of Quinwood

grandson, Troy George, was the church's pastor for many years. A great grandson of George Washington George, Aldon David George, was also licenced to preach by the church.

The First Baptist Church of Quinwood has sponsored many service programs for the town, including the Boy Scouts of America and the Girl Scouts of America. A church bus runs twice a week to pick up any area residents who have no way to attend church services. When ever there is a need in the community, the First Baptist Church of Quinwood responds, offering counseling and support, both spiritual and material.

In every generation since its founding, Quinwood has produced a higher than average number of young people who have become doctors, nurses, preacher, teachers, soldiers, sailors and marines. The need to serve their

Pvt. Ralph Eugene Pomeroy

fellow man seems as ingrained in the population as their love of the mountains in which they were born.

Ralph Eugene Pomeroy is a shining example of the young men and women of Quinwood. Ralph was born on March 30, 1930. He was a member of the United States Army, and served during the Korean War.

Private Pomeroy was a machine gunner with Company E, and during an enemy attack on October 15, 1952 he opened fire on the Korean troops, which slowed their advance and blunted the attack. The enraged soldiers concentrated all their weapons on Pvt. Pomeroy's position in order to neutralize his fire.

Pomeroy held his ground and continued to shoot until an enemy mortar wounded him and destroyed the mounting gear on his machine gun. Pomeroy then released the gun from its

Pvt. Roger Paul McDaniel

mount and picked up the hot, heavy weapon and ran forward, laying down a hail of bullets. He was wounded a second time, but did not stop. Just as Pomeroy reached the enemy troops, his gun ran out of ammunition. Rather than surrender, he used his gun as a club against his opponents until he was killed. His actions prevented his platoon from being overrun and allowed them to retain control over their perimeter.

Ralph Eugene Pomeroy was awarded the Medal of Honor and a Purple Heart for his extreme valor and supreme sacrifice, which was considered above and beyond the call of duty by the military. In 2001 a battle ship, the USNS Pomeroy was named in his memory.

A second heroic young man from Quinwood, Roger Paul McDaniel, gave his life in service of his country in Vietnam on July 6,

Mine Boss Shirley O'Dell Boone

1967. Roger was born on December 24, 1945 in Quinwood. He spent the early years of his childhood overcoming the devastating effects of polio. Roger was a private in the US Army and was serving with F Troop, Second Squadron in the 11th Armored Cavalry in Quang Tin, Vietnam when he was killed in action by an explosive devise. He was awarded the Purple Heart posthumously. The Roger McDaniel Memorial Sunday School Class at the First Baptist Church of Quinwood was named in his honor.

The town has been home to many influential citizens through the years. They include Shirley O'Dell Boone, Eugene (Geno) McKenzie and JoAnn Boone Clements.

Shirley Boone is remembered by locals not only for her dedicated service to the First Baptist Church of Quinwood, where she was a member and the church custodian for more than

Quinwood McKenzie Memorial Park Entrance

twenty years, but also because she was one of the earliest women in the state to become a coal miner. Shirley excelled at her job, and became the first woman in West Virginia to earn the right to be a boss in an underground coal mine.

Eugene (Geno) McKenzie was of Italian descent. His family moved to the coalfields in the Quinwood area because mining was one of the few places where immigrants could obtain work in America in the early 1900s.

Geno was born on June 26, 1928. He was a self made man who owned several coal mines over the years. He was also a contractor, a landlord and an entrepreneur. But he felt that his greatest accomplishment was the fact the he was able to offer employment to hundreds of West Virginians, so that they could support their families. Geno was a firm believer in education, and provided scholarships for many students in

JoAnn Boone Clements (Top Center) and Team

the Quinwood area. He donated land and money to the town on several occasions, including four acres that he gave to create a community park.

Named the McKenzie Memorial Park in his honor, the park has a performance stage, playground equipment, picnic shelters, a tennis court and a basketball court. Mr. McKenzie was also the Mayor for many years in the nearby town of Rainelle, and was active in many local organizations.

Quinwood's most renowned sports celebrity is JoAnn Clements, the daughter of Gary and Shirley Boone. JoAnn was a star basketball player during her school years at Greenbrier West High School and later at the University of Charleston.

In 1985, JoAnn was recruited for the women's barnstorming basketball team, 'The All

Quinwood Miner's Memorial Statue

American Redheads'. The all girl team was the female version of the 'Harlem Globetrotters', and was recently inducted into the Naismith Memorial Basketball Hall of Fame. JoAnn said of her time in the League *"It was fun. We traveled all over the United States and played ball. It was a real experience. You met a lot of people."*

During her time with the team, JoAnn played over 100 games. The Red Heads only played all men teams, often from the local police and fire departments or colleges. Each girl had a special talent that they displayed during half time at the game. JoAnn did a 'double dribble' with two basket balls. She also spun the ball on her finger, her knee, and her elbow, which she would use to shoot the ball into the hoop.

After retiring from the team, JoAnn eventually returned to college to earn her

Quinwood Memorial List of Coal Miners

prerequisites for nursing, and now provides private care for the elderly.

Few of the residents of the community are still actively involved in the coal mining industry, but they have not forgotten the roots of the former coal camp. In 2007 they raised enough donations to build a 'Coal Miners Memorial' to honor all of the coal miners from Quinwood and the surrounding areas.

Greenbrier County Delegate Tom Campbell spoke at the dedication ceremony for the memorial on June 30, 2007, saying *"The men and women of Quinwood and this area have known that life can be hard in the mountains, particularly working in the coal industry, but that life required hard work, persistence, dedication and loyalty; and they met that challenge."*

More recently, the community has

Quinwood Community Building

formed 'The Concerned Citizens of Quinwood and Vicinity, Inc'. The goal of the group is to 'put something back' into the community. When the WV Library Commission terminated funding for the Quinwood Library, they stepped in to keep the library open, and helped complete a one and a half mile walking trail for the town. Members if the group also maintain and equip the new Quinwood Community Building, which provides the townspeople with a meeting place.

Such dedication to service makes it clear that even after almost one hundred years, the Herald of Hope mission which began in the small coal camp in 1922 is still very much alive in Quinwood today.

At the end of their trip in 1995, Wilma and Norman Taylor visited the last known location of the Herald of Hope, on the railroad tracks where the Imperial Smokeless Coal

'Herald of Hope' Chapel Car

Company side railed it so long ago. Looking down at the site, Mrs. Taylor memorialized the chapel car when she said, *"Daylight is fading. You can see the lights from the homes in Marfance through the trees on the hill and hear the bustle on the darkening streets of Quinwood. From the night shadows of the valley below, you can almost smell oil lamps and see their glow through art-glass window trim. If you listen carefully, you can almost hear on the autumn breeze blowing - the sound of a hymn, vigorously, lovingly pumped on an Estey organ."*

Resources

Taylor, Wilma Rugh, and Taylor, Norman Thomas, *This Train is Bound for Glory: The Story of America's Chapel Cars*. 1999@Judson Press, Valley Forge, PA 19482-0851.

Nuttall, John. *Trees Above with Coal Below*. 1961@Neyenesch Printers, San Diego, CA.

Dulaney, Annie Harvey, *The Years of the Elk and Little Kanawha Railroad*, Braxton County Historical Society Journal - December 1976@hurherald.com.

America's Rail Road Chapel Cars, taken from the internet on Sept. 25, 2013, from http:en.wikipedia.org/Railroad_Chapel_car.

Walrath, Harry R. *God Rides the Rails: Chapel Cars on the Nations Railroads*, taken from the internet on Oct. 5, 2013 from http://www.frontiertrails.com/oldwest/chapel.html.

Myers, Anna Edith, *Churches on Wheels in the West*, taken from the internet on Oct 1, 2013 from ebooks@google.com.

Atkinson, Tommy, *The Charleston Gazette*, April 3, 2012, 'Red Heads' get call to Hall of Fame.

West Virginia Memory Project - Veterans Database, taken from the internet on Oct. 9, 2013 from

http://w.wvculture.org/history/wvmemory/vetdetail.aspx?Id=685.

Hunter, Troy, internet website at http://www.meadowbluff.com/

About the Author

Nancy Richmond is an award winning author who has been writing professionally for over thirty years, as a newspaper and magazine columnist and as the author of thirteen books. She is a lifelong resident of Greenbrier County, WV, and a member of the Greenbrier Historical Society and the West Virginia Writers Inc. Her books can be found at Tamarack in Beckley, at the North House Museum and the Open Book in Lewisburg, and at Amazon.com and numerous other book store sites on the internet.

Nancy attended Bluefield State College, and worked for Seneca Mental Health, Inc., and for the town of Quinwood as a police clerk, a town recorder and a municipal court judge. She is an avid dog fancier and has owned, bred and shown many AKC Champion dogs.

Nancy and her husband Charles, also an author, currently reside in Historic Lewisburg, West Virginia. For more information on the author and her books, please visit :

nancyrichmondbooks.com